Early Films

Early Films

Brenda Coultas

RODENT Press

Boulder, Colorado

Published July, 1996 in Boulder, Colorado
by Rodent Press, 303-440-8125

First edition

© Brenda Coultas, 1996

Cover photographs by Bob Gwaltney

The cover for *Early Films* was designed and letterpress printed by Brad O'Sullivan on the Kavyayantra Press at The Naropa Institute.

Some of these pieces have previously appeared in the following magazines: *Bombay Gin, Big Rain, Cyanosis, Mirage, The Little Magazine, Hayden's Ferry Review, Handy Jugs, News 4U, Pagen Place, Poetry Project Newsletter, Psalms 151, Westword, Singles Style, Slack, Sniper Logic, The New Censorship, The World,* and the Lip CD.

Multi-thanks for time and encouragement to Jane Morrow Below, Matt Corry, Jack Collom, Todd Colby, Elaine V. Coultas, Alison Dorfman, Beth Grace, Bob Gwaltney, Bobbie Louise Hawkins, Brad & Becky & Kevin & Debra Harris, Jennifer Heath, Laird Hunt, Judy Hussie, Darius James, Robert MacDaniel, Averil Paskow, Wang Ping, Eléni Sikélianòs, Bill Sovern & Grace Strange, Laurel Stone, Edwin Torres, Anne Waldman, Jo Ann Wasserman, and Kenji Yuda.

Early Films is available through SMALL PRESS DISTRIBUTION, 1814 SAN PABLO AVE., BERKELEY, CA 94702-1624, 510-549-3336.

ISBN: 1-887289-15-1

for Andy and Betty

contents

how i became a man   11
stones   12
eat   16
my life and my death   19
falcon   20
birth   23
dr. death   26
car   30
the love room   31
limb   35
basketball story   36
root   50
the spaces for lovers to live in   51
psychic camp   53
miriam   56
the rise of sex towards god   57
dream life in a case of transvestism   58
country   60
ostriches running   65
appendage   66
blackie   67
margaret   69
tinderbox   72
nature   76

how i became a man

      I learned to lean into them and open their legs and part their lips with the weight of my new body. I held their tiny palms inside the cups of my hands. I did not know their skin would be soft.

stones

On the top of the bank is where I began collecting rocks. I pushed the chunks of limestone and watched them roll down to the shoulder of the road. Some rocks were small enough to carry. The rock that smashed in Lulu's head was fist-sized.

In my room, the rocks are stacked underneath a mural of a waterfall. You cannot even tell they are weapons. They are arranged to look like the base of the fall. The rocks meander throughout the house in a stream that connects every room.

In the stream is a rock for every man that used to circle the house or call at three in the morning with a voice that said, "Everyone in a small town knows where the hen house is."

Lulu went with the callers who knew the right codes and she would wear her best underwear. On nights when the hang-up calls were heavy she turned out the lights and took my hands, singing, "We are the chickens in the hen house, the foxes, circle and circle, looking for a crack in the fence, an opening door to rush at," and she sang faster and faster until we fell down like ring-around-the-rosie.

One night before I began to collect weapons, a man came in through a cracked window while I was drunk and passed out on my bed. Lulu came home and pelted him with shoes until he ran out of the house and down the street past the other shotgun houses. She woke me up and we walked outside. Can collectors were picking up my high heels. It looked like the sky rained shoes all over the street. I am still missing a strapless silver sandal.

When we were drunk and the car quit on us, we found this place on the bank. It was cold and rainy and we had on short skirts. We climbed up to the bank to squat by a bush. We peed, but then kept going to the top of the bank, to the top of the rip rap, where the limestone reflected the street lights. We thought this must be what the moon looks like. It was a place to be safe in, not like home where prowlers turn the knob and thrust their full weight against the door. There we were safe and had weapons to hurl through the air. Weapons to throw. We made axes from green branches and stones. We could have become lovers. After her death, my nails grew and curled under.

Lulu was found lying on the path we used to take through the rip rap, where our high heels wedged between the limestone chunks. She was naked except for a short skirt that was laid over her hips like a tablecloth.

My rope was around her neck. The rope we used to tie a tire on the bumper of my old wrecked car so we could push it home. It was not used for anything unclean like her work in the bus station and the shop.

I ran the projector and she never complained about the movies being out of focus and the sticky seats. She was the whore of our lobby. She stood in the shadows waiting for men. One time I had a broken heart and she ordered a pizza for me. She said she had no heart of gold like movie whores. She said, "My heart is a diamond. It is a beautiful stone."

A week after her murder, the police sent me donuts wrapped up in a composite drawing of my face. They picked me up and drove me around. They shot a stray dog "to save the dog pound work." They took me to the policeman's club and gave me a beer. They said, "Drink, drink, we bought this beer for you." They took my shoes off and poured beer on my toes and licked it off. They showed me their weapons and drank out of my shoes and said, "We like leather." I tried to leave before they got my shirt off. They said, "You can't leave. This beer is full." I tricked them and poured it out when they weren't looking. When they got drunk enough I ran away.

I was brought in for questioning by a detective that I saw dancing under the club's mirror ball. He took me to a room with a mirror I could see through when I cupped my hands together and pressed up against it. He sat down across from me and read my rights. He said, "You're here because you could have killed her."

He drank from a chipped cup that had a buildup of coffee stain and his nails were short and jagged. These were the things I looked at because I could not bring my eyes up. I looked at the layer of tobacco smoke on the fake mirror and the little brown grooves burned into the table. These were the things I concentrated on. "Why do you suspect me?" I asked. "Was she not killed viciously enough?" I remembered the women in the books I found left behind in the theater. Stained books with pages stuck together that I brought into the light of my projection booth. Picture books of women made into lamps and furniture. A woman's bones boiled clean and made into an easy chair and another woman swinging from a hook like a country ham. "Where did you get that rope?" he said.

He drove me home in a car without passenger handles. I wondered about jail. Would I have to let the cell block mamas eat me out? Would I like it? Lulu said that our love would not be like love made for the movies where the man pulls out and everything is made sticky. She said our love would not be made for cameras or any other eyes.

I walk to work. My work is the unwinding and rewinding of reels of pantiless maids, butlers, doctors and housewives all bending over and starting orgies.

I keep going until the street lights end and I am alone and safe. Only then I can open up the weapon I've made of my heart, a blue flint that when struck produces sparks, flame and ash.

eat

Here is my neck. Here is his leg. His leg swollen like a river. Look at his great truck. Look at his wide body full on the bed. Father's father is a headstone of fathers and mothers.
Here a rock. Here a pebble.
A penny
A limestone
A granite
Here a plate of minerals.

Here a gold tooth.
Here a basalt.
Here a salt block and cow tongue.

Here you be there I be buried here and there.

In Lillydale, flows a milk stream of tears. A fine broth of tears and salt (father's father you have made a fine soup here, you've made me a kettle of fish I can't refuse). Your fish is delicious fine bones and firm white.

Your fish I ate into a shape, I ate your fish into a comb. I stroke my hair now. I groom myself with oil. I rake my hair in place. I ate your fish into a boat. I sail away now. I think I'm in the belly of a whale, I'm in a cave, I think I'm a caveperson I think I'm drawing on walls. All of my writing is being written by another.

(I'm in your (a) river. I'm in your (a) mad ocean.)

Deafness, here.
Please work for the night is coming.

Here is my neck, I'm putting it away now (in trunk). I'm putting it away now.

A fine broth of salt wears away the stone. Your statue is fading away. Your fine face falls.

His stone wore away into a lump of coal.

The lambs on the child's stone are gone now dissolved by tears. They walked away of their own accord. I opened the gate. First they grazed as always not realizing that a hole had opened up. They followed the richest grass, it led them out.

I tempered them one by one.

Look at my neck of rare construction, it was broke into. I said yes, it's new again, the doctor made it new again. A construct of turkey bones. A construct of a kite: balsa wood and moleskin,
I'm flying now, Every time the wind picks up I'm flying again. Mother I'm flying now.

recite long string of names here. (list of family names and random titles)

The little blue room was pink.

The room changed from pink to blue.

I'm eating you into a shape. I've eaten you into an animal cracker. I'm eating off the rough edges. I'm making shape, I making a smooth shape, I'm evening out the edges now. I'm planning the surface. I'm eating you into a smooth round coin.

Father, please be still!

my life and my death

The killing spree occurs because postal workers are required by law to make bad fashion statements. The black socks with shorts. Who can blame them? Why not the nice brown of the UPS persons or the pleasant khaki of zoo personnel.

In *How to Avoid Killing Sprees by Postal Employees,* the author cites the color blue as the causation factor a catalyst or trigger finger. The blue uniforms (particularly in that tone) repress aggression like a tea kettle without a vent. All that repression is restrained within the chest, groin and thighs; is air not circulated, is skin not breathing is blue as a vein over and under the skin running through the body caged and contained pushing at the walls to find the weak spot to allow release to break in the dam become a flood become waves crashing, a wall of red and blue rushing and then still. This could all be solved by painting the post offices vulva pink.

falcon

She was driving a 67 falcon black with red interior. She had gone too far with boys, her mother said, "girls like you are ate up and spit out everyday."

She had to pick up the boy. She had the only car that was running.

The boy was on his way to special school. His hair was long and shiny and his teeth stained from purple gum. The boy had a knife. He opened it up and cut the dirt from his nails. The cb radio made a constant crackle, an intermittent good buddy, 10-4 breaker breaker. She said "My handle is Bewitched. Do you have a handle?"

"No," he said. "Just Crank, You can guess how I got that name. My friend Speed christened me."

Crank had a hunk of gum in his mouth. A wad of psychedelic bubble gum, a round ball of gum in bright colors. Everything was called psychedelic that year.

The radio said "Good Buddy."

"I gotta get some money Crash owes me before I head back to school. Who knows I may not even go at all. It's a bunch of shit anyways."

In the dark of the ashtray sat a pair of hemostats.

A girl in school went too far with a boy and had to drop out. Everyone believed that she had moved to another state. It turned out she'd been at home the whole time. She'd seen everyone come and go during the year. They made her give the baby away or maybe she really didn't want it, you know.

The boy said."Have some gum."
He held out a piece the size of a pencil eraser.

Two girls named Polly and Molly went too far. They were found in a drainage ditch. On their way home from a pj party, they met two boys in a park, who drank beer and fucked them. The boys killed Polly and Molly afterwards so they couldn't tell. A girl shouldn't tell said all the girls in her group. No one should squeal on anyone.

She was in an old trailer with a boy. It was actually an abandoned school bus in a woods. Inside was a stove with a little smokestack plunging through the roof. There was one school bus seat. The cover was ripped and horse hair spilled out. There were posters on the walls with big blocky letters that waved when you looked at them too long. Someone had tried to hang out there. You could tell by the way it was decorated with posters and bean bag chairs. A set of orange plastic cups with mushrooms decals rested on a shelf.

Every time the falcon topped the hill the radio came in stronger. The falcon said, "Good buddy, what's your 10-20?"

In the glove box was a half eaten tablet of miltown wrapped in tissue and a cookie. She licked the sides to make it last.

The boy ate the miltown. It made him just barely sleepy.

A little knife went click click.

Things in a car: rolling papers, an STP patch, stickers: *War is not good for children and other living things*, *Ban Homework*, *Down with School Lunches*. Thick clay beads on a strip of rawhide, a puka shell necklace, fake turquoise, a dull sky blue set in pot metal filagree, a roach clip with feathers, a t-shirt with a glitter decal, a small tarry bong, old movie still poster and a short film clip of Johnny Wadd.

to Averil, thanks for the 70's

birth

In her bedroom, Beth places a part of herself on the shelf next to a skull ashtray and an 8-ball. She is not allowed out of bed as her stitches haven't healed. She is fifteen and weighs ninety pounds instead of one hundred and fifteen. She used to worry about being pregnant but now she wonders if she'll ever be able to fuck again.

Before I knew I was sick I thought I was pregnant.

I played the patient and laid out naked under a sheet on the kitchen table. My two boyfriends played doctors and examined me with their instruments. They wore condoms made of plastic bags from my mother's junk drawer. Afterward, I began to feel pain. It was like being cut inside with a sharp knife. I threw myself over chairs hoping to kill it, but that only made the pain worse. I was in such pain that I had to tell my mother. My pain was greater than fear. She took me to a doctor who saw the teeth in my stomach. The teeth were in a ball of hair and skin that floated in my belly. He pointed to the space above it. "This is the problem," he said.

"I didn't want to know," her mother said. "Beth hadn't been eating and was dizzy and sick. I thought she was pregnant and that her life would be ruined because she is so young. I thought she was having sex because she shaved her legs and pierced her ears without my permission. They develop so early now, what with vitamins and hormones in the meat — the chicken I fried every Sunday after church. Every day in South America six year old girls grow armpit hair.

When the doctor told me about the thing inside her, I was relieved because it was not sin that caused it. I felt guilty. My body passed this on to her. It was another child. It should have been a sister, or a brother for her to play with. Was I drinking too much coffee or wine? We didn't know about those things then, that drinking and smoking made problems. We didn't think about 'fetuses.'"

My church tried to raise money to save it as they felt that all of life is sacred. The pastor said, "Even cancer wants to grow, your body is a vehicle for life." He said, "If you let them remove it you'll go to hell. When it was removed I worried about hell, but I was myself again and not the carrier of another being.

Beth kept the fetus and showed her friends, who had heard of women giving birth to space aliens and lungfish but never to a ball of hair.

One night in her bedroom the part of her that was removed began to speak.

"I remember how we started. We were a whisper between our parents, under covers, in the dark, beside the lit candle, by the bed.

God saw that their love was good and gave us to them. Love always calls for a sacrifice. Remember our mother pushing us into the world. I was born with you, in you. I made small and ate your body. I floated above everything. I am a fish pulled from the waters of your ocean. I have no name in this new world. I speak. My teeth gnash in the thin air so words can be heard. I am hair, teeth and skin. I whisper with language I learned underwater. My name for you is Sister-Mother. I have no eyes, you are my eyes. Look at me. I am proof of sea monsters. A sea monster climbed with fins up walls and locked on to your center."

Beth threw the fetus on the floor, breaking it. She swept it up, put it in a jar, put the jar in the closet.

Beth, who is eighteen, nearly a woman now, thinks of all the objects she has placed into her vagina: vibrators, sponges, spermicides.

She sees herself with others in a circus tent, seated behind a velvet rope. They are all dressed in sheets that they raise up one by one. A third leg protruded through one chest wall. A twin dangled from between another's legs. Beth sees herself hold up her sheet and show her scar.

She is as primitive as a coelacanth long thought extinct until pulled from deeper, older waters with the ghosts of its toes still intact.

dr. death

There are two Dr. Deaths in my life. My boyfriend is one. He calls himself "Dr. Death." He kills in the thousands daily and on better days he kills in the tens of thousands. He annihilates generations. He drives the company truck home with its big plastic detachable bug on top. We remove it at night unless we feel adventurous. Then we leave it on and knock on people's doors and pretend they're our customers. They let us in and as we inspect the baseboards for crevices they say, "We don't remember calling the exterminator." We try to get invited for dinner. We touch things and compliment them on their clean habits that keep their bugs puny and vulnerable to disease.

After he goes to work in the morning, I imagine him in his uniform opening cabinet doors and pulling the stuffing out of old refrigerators and training a flashlight beam on their dark greasy nests. I think of women shrinking when a roach leaps off a door frame or of apartments where they rustle behind the wallpaper and of the soft crunch under a bare sole.

He knew I needed him. When we first met, my apartment had the most virile roaches he had ever seen.

My boyfriend is an honest man. He never takes anything of value from his customers and he told me his other girl friends left him to become lesbians. I assure him that he is not the cause, for he is a generous lover.

They were women in transition and he helped to free them.

    The other Dr. Death calls himself "Lewis" and he waits for me at work behind the north side of the building. I call him Dr. Death because he is a meat packer at a processing plant. He said he never tires of meat even though he makes it every day and when he wears his white processing jacket with its faint grime of blood on the cuffs and neck, he looks like a surgeon. He sits in his truck and watches the men who park along the levee wall that runs beside the building.

    Behind the wall everything is coated with a film from the backwater of the river that rises and falls throughout the year. The men mow paths and lay out on sheets in the weeds sometimes, just like at the drive-in when you bring a blanket and lay out on the hood. They leave notes pinned down with rocks, notes that say, "I want to suck you hard and dry." There are notes for the hairy chested and large men and some notes are addressed to "the finder."

    Lewis walks the mowed trails and pretends to be a cop. He carries a long, black flashlight. At night with my flashlight, I spotlight the row of men and watch them withdraw from their embraces. I spotlight them to get them to move on.

    The police have found dead ones back there in those bushes. Nude ones, nude to keep them from running for help. Men from out of town are murdered, men from those tiny, clean perfectly laid out squares where the relatives of the victims are always puzzled by the circumstances of the murder. In the newspapers the wife says, "I don't know what he was doing there."

    Lewis wants to talk to me about the weirdos who hang out back there and I want to say, "You are a weirdo too for watching them have sex," but I remain mute for he would reply that he's not breaking the law, they are. My boyfriend knows about him and he is not jealous. He is only jealous of other women.

At work, Lewis calls me from my rounds of the perimeter fence. He says, "Come here I want to show you something." We walk behind the wall and I follow him on a freshly cut path that ends in a thicket of weeds. Lewis parts them with his flashlight and reveals a fissure that we follow until weeds close over our heads.

"Here," he says. "Someone has been living in the weeds back here."

They have been living in a box, one that reads, "Keep This City Clean." Inside the box is a blanket and a brown sack. I poke the sack with a stick, and nothing moves. It is lightweight, not heavy like flesh or fluid would be. It is not a baby or a dead dog.

The sack is filled with photos. The photos are of a wedding but they are scraps, the mistakes.

The photos are out of focus and some are test strips with a spectrum of color across them. There are five copies of one certain picture of the bride alone, smiling into the eye of the camera.

Around the box the weeds are matted down but there is no sign of struggle or human waste. There is nothing in the box to give a clue as to who is living in it. None of the photos are nude.

Lewis grips his flashlight and says, "I've been watching this box, looking for who's living in it. I think queers are living in it."

I tell my boyfriend about the box and he says that he has never seen a box person, only shopping cart people. He believes that living in a box would be better, but not as safe. He makes a package and fills it with a jar of bee pollen and honeycomb that he took from the health food store he sprays. In this week's newspaper no one has been murdered or reported missing.

My boyfriend and I take the package and walk into the weeds and the weeds are as dense as water. As we walk we see movement, movement in the weeds from the men walking and seeking each other. The box is the same as before only now the blanket has been wadded into a pillow and on the pillow there are a few notes from men seeking teenage love. We leave a note that reads: To whoever lives here this food is safe, take it and eat it, all of it.

At work, Lewis calls me over to the row of cars along the wall. He is holding a note that he slips into his white jacket and says he saw us today and he will watch the box for us.

In the morning, we return and the weeds yield to us. We find the box and it has been dismembered and the remains are strewn throughout the weeds. The honey has been poured out and flies are drowning in it. There is a bag resting on the blanket and we can hear things rattling through the paper. I rip the bag with a long stick and the flies swarm out. They have been eating a chunk of meat.

car

I got into a car with a stranger. He asked me to blow him. I said, "Okay, for a Coke." This didn't seem strange to me at the time even though what I really wanted was a Diet Pepsi.

the love room

There is a spiritualist church on the corner of 2nd and Oak. It is a small building with red asphalt siding and a white wooden steeple. Jane sits on a pew and waits for the minister to arrive and ask questions of the dead. She wants to talk with her grandmother, but isn't sure if she should bother her. Even though they had been close in life, her grandmother might not love her now that she was above the world and could see all of Jane's sins. But, she didn't know any other dead people only the famous dead and everyone claimed to channel them.

Since her grandmother died she has become nervous. The nervousness has insidious forms: it is a shakiness in her bones, a companion, a topic among her friends.

At first she thought it was a brain tumor or diabetes but the doctors ran tests and said no.

Her hands have shaken since birth. She waited for the nervousness as her mother and grandmother had. They would lay in bed on sunny days waiting for it to pass. Each Saturday, they drove twenty miles to the drug store, hurrying before it closed so they would have enough pills for Sunday.

Her mother takes white chunks, her grandmother had taken small blue dots and Jane takes pink ovals.

The pills keep her from pinching or burning herself or wearing tight shoes so that she can feel her feet but the pills can not prevent her from watching her mother's chest rise and fall at night. It is the only way she can tell her mother is not dead.

She had to learn to let thoughts of poison, cancer, brain tumors, disease, capsules packed with cyanide and the perfume of bitter almonds given off by large vats of spiked Kool-Aid ride through her body. The thoughts ride on waves of her body's electricity. They spark and fry. She has learned by reading books, to let it come and expend itself.

When she thinks hard she remembers when as a girl, she had to say everything three times as a safeguard against bad luck. Another time she imagined bugs in her mouth and spit till her mouth ached, and still felt the lumps in her throat. Then she thought of the most horrible tortures that one person could do to another, and she prayed for things to be all right until she fell asleep at night hoping God would watch over the world and not judge her.

At the museum, she works in the animal room. Above the door is a brass plate with the name of the benefactor, Mr. Perkins, inscribed upon it. He became rich building roads and bridges after the war. He went on safaris and collected whole families of animals because he loved nature and felt closest to it indoors where he could share it with others. Mr. Perkins kept a detailed diary of his collection and it lay under glass in the center of the room.

The room is a replica of his hunting lodge with walnut paneling and the heads of exotic beasts mounted upon walnut plaques. The animals are protected from dust and sunlight by heavy glass cases and thick blinds. Jane's job is to tell people about the relationship between Mr. Perkins and art and nature.

In the church, the deacon gives her a blank square of paper and tells her to write the name of her dead and a question she wants to ask. She writes her grandmother's name and "Do you still love me?"

The deacon collects the papers and takes them to the pulpit. Overhead is a picture suspended from the ceiling. The picture is of an angel watching two children chase butterflies along the edge of a cliff. The angel is a giant with wings and a white tunic. The psychic is a large man with a jelly-roll hairstyle. He says he lost his wife in a car wreck and that brought him back to the Lord.

When he is finished speaking, the deacon hands him a blindfold. The psychic holds it up and asks if anyone wants to try it on. He places two silver coins in the cloth where his eyes will be and ties the blindfold. He picks up a paper square from the basket and rubs it in his hair. His hair sticks up. He yells out. "Is someone going to Florida next week? I see a car. A red car. A chevy being packed with clothes."

A man yells back, "It's me, we are going Friday."

"Is your name Jack?" Said the psychic.

"Yes."

"Your brother Harold says that everything will be okay. You don't think so now, but it will be so."

The psychic said, "I get pictures in my head and they flee very fast. If you don't say yes, they go even faster. The dead show me pictures."

"Jane Morrow," he yells, "I see a bed being made and the covers being pulled back. Was she sick?"

"Yes," Jane steadied her weight on the back of the pew. "Does she love me still?"

"No. He said, "She is shaking her head no."

After the service, Jane talked to other people, including a channeler and all of them believe the psychic is real. She pinches her arms and says to the nervousness, "I am yours, take me. The dead are watching us and sit in judgement."

At the museum it is the slow season. All the grade school tours are over. Jane is in the animal room, or the love room as she likes to call it, because Mr. Perkins loved his animals enough to preserve them. She opens the blinds and the sunlight falls on a wild boar. In the bright light she can see that the hide is split and cracked open. She pulls the blind and it rips. She falls backward and the boar with his painted gums still pink, his polished teeth and broken skin stands above her and he seems to be saying, "I am your love."

limb

The top of the leg was hard plastic hollowed out to fit the stump of the upper thigh. The lower leg and calf sections were made of metal with an adjustable hinge in the middle acting as the knee. The bottom was detailed like a large doll's foot with the plastic toes webbed together. I wanted to buy the leg but there was no price tag on it. I touched the outside and peered down the hollow core. The inside was dark and stained. The intimacy repulsed me. I couldn't bring myself to purchase the leg so I committed the details to memory.

basketball story

A man keeps two women, naked and bound, as prisoners in his attic. He likes to touch their bodies with an instrument he made himself. An electric cord with clamps on the end.

His girlfriend lives next door with their children. Her name is Charlene and she helps him feed and bathe the women. Every other day, after she makes supper for the children, she leads each woman to her bath. The women are blindfolded with hands tied in back.

These are not the only ones. The first woman, he released into a corn field in the middle of the night. He had kept her in the first prison, a hollowed out crawl space under the house.

The hamburgers Charlene cooks for the prisoners are made from old beef, patties mashed out and served on white bread. Sometimes with corn chips or whatever the children didn't eat. She cleans the women with dishwashing soap and a garden hose. She would be glad when he got tired of them. Then it would be just her and him again, not those other faces and bodies.

Another man in town takes boys riding in his van. He drives to a barn where he experiments. He grafts the remains of the freshest boys together. He has all the parts required to make a new boy but no freezer to preserve them in.

In this town are two smells that rise from the bakery factory. In the morning, the smell of cakes baking, in the evening, the smell of ammonia used to clean the cake pans.

Clyde drowned his fiancée in a lake because she was pregnant. He tried to make it look like a boating accident. He was caught and went to death row where he lives behind a steel door. The door has a slot for receiving food. Through the slot comes messages hidden beneath the trays from the other prisoners. The messages say, "How is the food? Read any good books lately? Are you lonely? You look good to me?" He pushes the empty trays back through the slot. There is a small window in the door with crossed bars. Each bar is laid over the top of the other, reducing the space. His girlfriend's spirit slides through spaces the size of spaghetti.

The men searched the lake for her. They dipped long poles with hooks into the water.

On a steel table she was laid out, beautiful and damp. On a tray laid the scalpels and saws: clean and sharp, new and shiny. The shells of her fingertips were cut off and inked. The coroner arranged them in rows like a stamp collection.

Christen has seen various women led through her father's house into the upstairs where only her mother and father are allow to go. She calls them her Aunts. Aunt Leah, Aunt Karen, Aunt Susie. She masturbates with the wooden handle of a hammer. She thinks, is this what sex is like? Will it be good? Will I like it?

She places a mirror between her legs and asks, "Is this the hymen? It this the clit? What are the names of my parts?" She reads medical books and looks at drawings overlaiden with clear pages; plastic printed with colors, pink and grey lungs, liver, spleen, and kidneys. She flips the layers of parts between her fingers. Looking for her parts, for what is outside, visible, and hidden.

She has learned not to talk, not to ask questions. Her words flow into an underground stream where they are protected from her mother and father. From reading she has learned the organs of speech: The back of the tongue, the blade of the tongue, the root of the tongue, the food passage, epiglottis, hard palate, soft palate, teeth and teeth ridge. She knows how the voice box opens and closes, but knows not to use it.

The police follow the man who kills boys. They drive a plain car. Inside the car is a red bubble light that plugs into the cigarette lighter. In the trunk are boxes for evidence, a roll of yellow tape that reads "Do Not Cross," and various kinds of cameras.

The killer works in a convenience store. He was once robbed by a man with a baseball bat. This makes him wary of the car that sits across the street each evening. He knows there are two people in the car because he sees the glow of two cigarettes.

He tries to see past the glare created by the store's inside lights. He plans what to do when the robbers come. If it's a robber with a knife, he will strike him with the wood axe he keeps behind the counter. In his mind is an equation: Knife = axe handle, strike stomach. Strike neck, knees or forearm. Robber with gun = Blind with insecticide spray. Grab gun. Pull back the thumb.

An Account of An Unsolved Murder 1979

There were these people and their names were Betty and Red. We met them when we moved into Wilma's Trailer Park. They're kinda, I don't know how to explain it. They're all mentally slow. They've lived rough lives, and hard lives. We're talking about carrying guns around and heavy drinking and running with real rough people. Her sister was kind of a rough person and she was married to this man who reminds me of a slug or I don't know but he's real slimy. She owed a lot of money to drug dealers and had some drugs out on consignment, and she never did come up with the money to pay it off. Anyway, one night while her husband was at home watching the kids, she went out to Dairy Queen and never came home and they found her body out in a field and she had been shot in the back of the head.

Well, her husband, I think his name was Ronnie, somehow he knew her dying words. The words she said right before she was shot. They found cans of beer where people had been drinking, like they were having a party. They thought she had been lured out there on the pretense of a party going on.

They also thought maybe he had been threatened by the drug dealers and he lured her out there and they took care of her. The way he did his beer cans was he bent them a certain way so that other people wouldn't drink out of them, or so he'd always know which were his at a party. All the cans out there were bent like that. But they have never found out anymore evidence on her murder. All they know is that she was last seen at the Dairy Queen.
End

The grave diviner measures off the field in squares. In each hand he holds a willow branch. He has found graves so old that only the coffin handles are left. Between the handles is rich, dark dirt. The rod in his left hand bends. He begins to dig until he reaches a plastic bag. He opens it up and inside is a bitch and her puppies. He has found a pet cemetery.

On this side of town, there are little shacks built on stilts by the river. They are built on ash heaps. The yards are decorated with tires that rise up slowly out of the soil. The tires are painted red and made to resemble giant tulips. All the buried trash rises to the top and is turned into lawn ornaments.

Christen knows what the unborn look like. She sees them on TV. She is filled with babies, tiny babies the size of gumballs lie in her stomach, shifting their weight each time one is released and comes out as blood. She knows that the babies are released by boys. Somehow boys are causing babies to be released in her underwear.

The television show with real murders features a man called the Highway Killer who shoots store clerks in the head. He doesn't even buy gum or anything before, not even a cold pop. He just shoots them and runs away. The show asks everyone to turn in possible murderers. They have three thousand suspects but the police think they can narrow it down in no time.

We owe several hundred dollars, will you help us get rid of this debt? In Phillippians the 4th chapter, verse 19, "My God shall supply all your needs in glory by Christ Jesus." God does that to you good people that give love offerings to his work. So send some love offerings today. God says owe no man nothing. That if I am the candle of the Lord, the bible says I am, I give light, in the darkness of this world, a hope for the future also. So what we need to do is to keep lighting that light. Strive for perfection in Christ. Let us increase our vocabulary in God by night.

Ellen's prison is a long narrow room. She is chained to the steel posts of the bed frame. She has lost track of the days and the rapes. She has now been here long enough for him to trust her. He has unbound her eyes, ears, arms, and mouth.

Next to the bed is a glass of water. In the glass of water she sees her mother, a tall thin woman. Her mother's face is lined and flat. Through the glass, she sees her mother walking through the rooms of their house. She wanders from room to room with clothes in her arms. Ellen's bedroom floats to the top of the water, her bed with pink roses on the borders. Her mother is laying down the clothes, sitting on the edge of her bed like when she had a fever.

"I'm fifteen," she says over and over. "My name is Ellen Lisa Mays. I must remember who I am. Who am I?" She asks herself and answers, "I'm Ellen Marie Mays."

I am fifteen. I live on third street. I belong to my mother Roberta Ann and to my father Leland Marcus Mays. I like to sew and fish. I was on my way to the market to get milk.

She tells him, the murderer of women, about who she is and why he must return her. What she misses. Her badges for merit and courage. Round cloth circles. One for campfires, one for cooking, a badge with a cake embroidered on it. She misses fishing. The town is built on the river. She and her brother went fishing every day during the summer. She collects worms. In the garage she kept a tin can full, at least a hundred worms all sliding over and over the dirt clod in the center. She thinks, no one knew about them but me. They are all dried up by now.

She remembers visiting an old slave house on a school trip. The house was a mansion on a hill. The attic ran the full length of the house. It had cells built into the sides that held bunk beds with no room to stand up in just enough space to get in bed and stay there. There was one large cell for women and children. In the center of the attic was a whipping post. The guide said the house was haunted.

Now I live in an attic chained to a bed. Other women have come and gone. He said there's no use feeding them anymore. When they left there would be the noise of chains and screams. Then quiet and they never came back. He comes in all day long with food and presents. One day, he gave her a small box. She opened it and inside was a finger. He has given her a locket, heart shaped. He fastened it around her neck.

He writes her love letters and writes his own reply back. "I love you," he says and she repeats his words back to him. She asks to leave and promises to return.

She has seen another girl here. A skinny girl with long blond hair, wearing a dress. She has seen her from the corners of her eyes. A girl on the stairs. The girl stands on the third stair. She thinks the girl is part of a recurring dream. A vision. "Is it myself I see?" she wonders. Each day, the girl advances another step up. She is a slowly rising apparition.

In the basement, Christen has began to collect things. She has: a pair of white high heels, a ring with a blue birthstone and bits of hair scraped off the ends of her father's shovel.

At the spiritualist church, the healers hold a seance. There is a cabinet from which the spirits enter and drop gifts on the crowd. They drop trinkets made of silver and stones bound together by locks of hair. One medium makes a precipitation portrait. He places a blank canvas under a sheet and meditates over it. He removes the cloth and a picture develops from fine dust, the color and texture of butterfly wings.

The picture is of the landscape between the two worlds, of planets rising above the trees and in colors not seen in nature on earth. His work hangs in a gallery made from an old trailer. The hallways inside the trailer glow with light from between this world and the next.

The other mediums do healing with stones and for an offering they will diagnosis an aura from saliva on a piece of cotton. They think of prosperity and prosperity comes to them. They ask the dead to speak and the dead speak through their throats. They can see angels, some without faces. The angels are made of light.

"How can you distinguish good angels from bad?"
"You know when you are in the presence of God."

The killer of boys is Carl. Carl carries a hunting knife with a bone handle. The blade is six inches long. He carries tools in a van customized for his work: tape, rope, a sharpening stone, and a gas stove for camping. He works in a triangle. The triangle formed by the three roads he travels on. All the killings that happen there belong to him. His killings are so clean he hardly has to change clothes.

"He beats me but not like in the beginning when it was daily," said Charlene. "His mother told me that he had bad brains. I didn't know what she meant at first. He was shy. I had to show him I was safe. He was like a wild horse. I held my hand out, palm open, and waited for him to come to me."

"It took a while before I knew about the others. I began to realize that food was missing and he was away every night. At Easter, he stole the whole ham. I found out but I still love him. Cause he can be sweet and I was afraid he'd kill me too."

Christen carves a city out of dirt for her dolls. She carves out houses and garages for the doll cars. She builds roads with tunnels, arches and gardens for a city of dolls. She cuts the hair of her favorite. A blonde with hair that is lengthened by pulling it out the top of the head. She has opened up the insides and found the source of hair. It begins in the belly, travels up the chest and neck and comes out the scalp.

Clyde has Roberta inside him; swallowed like a tablet resting in his stomach. A little heavy lump. This is where the dead go, they go inside of the living.

There are other men in the death house. Across from Clyde is a man who killed strangers. He placed bottles of poisoned aspirin, the tablets thick and swollen, on the shelves of drugstores. On the eve of each execution, curtains are drawn across the cells. Trays are returned untouched. The lights dim, then brighten. In his dreams he wears the outfit of the executed: black pants, white collarless shirt, gray socks and felt slippers. He is walking down a corridor lined with doors going until he comes upon the room, the chair with cloth straps and wired hat. It is a room with windows all around. It is a cage for electricity.

The lake was quiet, only the calls of birds broke the air. The only thing Clyde remembers clearly is striking her with the oar. A voice inside his head said row away and he did. A flash of dress, white, then gone. Her straw hat floats. It is a strange buoy resting on the quiet surface of the lake.

Death knocks on Carl's window; the north window that looks out over the alley. Her face is a half moon, one side bright. The other dark. Her only visible hand is a hook, curled up in perpetual invitation. (A gesture to move towards.) From his bed, the covers pulled up tight and neat, Carl is awakened, sits up and watches. Her knocking is soft, a faint echo among the sound of insects. She has been coming to him for a long time. The first time he met her, he had fallen through the ice while skating. Beneath its surface, in the cold water, he began to dream. It was warm and he wanted to sleep. He saw her and took hold of her outstretched hook. He began to rise. Was pulled up despite the great weight of his boots and jacket. He was a heavy fish, a great bass in this pond, rose against his will and broke the surface. His eyes opened, the hook was the hand of his brother. His brother carried him to the fire, gave him hot chocolate and rubbed the blood back into Carl's hands and feet.

Charlene goes shopping for soap and toilet paper with the coupons that fall from between the pages of the Sunday News. Usually she forgets and leaves them at home stacked up on the windowsill, expiring and fading in the sun. She straps the youngest child into the safety seat of the cart and drives it down the aisles. She buys pink dish soap, scouring pads, bacon, eggs, bread and silver duct tape. She buys enough food for herself, him, the kids and the women.

Ellen's mother lights a candle every night. It is a candle for the cursed. A wish candle for those unlucky in love, finance and luck. One side reads WISHES & DREAMS, FAITH & HOPE, RUN DEVIL RUN. She thinks to herself, a desperate measure for desperate people. Burning it reminds her of a cave grotto she saw. The lit candles in the same tall, fat jars and long match sticks for reaching the deep wicks. Outside the grotto was a spring struck from a rock by a sister of mercy. People filled old milk jugs with the water. She watched a woman splash the water on her face and hands. She filled up a paper cup and drank it and threw the cup out the window on the way home.

This morning, the young girl appeared at the foot of the bed. Ellen reached the end of her chain. The girl remained just out of range. She dropped a doll at Ellen's feet and left. The doll was bald. Its trunk was split open and filled with folded squares of toilet paper. Inside the right leg was a fossil. In the trunk was a white chalky mint. The arms contained bits of colored glass, the head held a razor blade. The edge of it protected by heavy paper.

The first victim was a blond who wore blue jeans with the knees unraveled into long threads. He picked him up on the highway. They drove to an open field.

He hit him in the head with an old police slapper. It was black leather and hand stitched. He sliced him with a box cutter. He used to slice himself. Cut lines across his arms. All up and down. The blood would lie on top. The blood pooled up and dried there.

The blonde didn't die. He crawled to the blacktop. He was missing skin from the back and thighs. The only thing he had on was a cowboy hat.

Carl keeps a record of his dreams. He sends them off in the mail to a dream interpreter.

Dear Dream Lady, I dreamt I murdered a little boy. I try to draw a picture of the murder. I can draw the bodies, but I cannot draw the faces. The faces are a blank. In the dream I see the back of someone who I know is me. I cannot see for sure what is happening. But the person who is me turns around and the boy falls to the floor at his feet. What does this mean?

Dear Dreamer, To dream about murder indicates you do not want interference from that person. You don't really want to kill. A dream that you are murdered is a desire to be released from a hardship.

Wishing you a good night.
Dream Lady

His diary is pink with a rose on the cover. It has a tiny lock and key that he wears on a string around his neck. He has learned to relax his throat muscles, to drop the key down the food passage and let it dangle. When he does this it makes him think of a story about a man who snored with his mouth open. One night a hungry rat crawled down his throat and tore out a hunk of flesh. After that Clyde kept his lips hidden under the covers at night.

A picture of Carl by the grill in the back yard of his mother's house. It is dark. A long spatula in his hand. In the corner of the frame are his mother's feet clad in blue slippers.

The crystal gazers lay out their tools to purify. They lay out clear quartz and wands made of wood and crystal held together with leather and decorated with feathers. They are letting the stones leach out impurities. Each evening they pray over a map of the United States. They have the whole country covered except for Alaska and Hawaii.

On TV Christen saw a man make a hole in a woman with his hands and pull out hard knots of flesh. He said some magic words and the hole closed up. The woman smiled, got up and walked away. That is what my father does. He opens up the body and takes away the bad spots. I've seen him cut off the bad parts before. I saw him cut off fingers one at a time.

What was inside that hole? I have babies in my body, feeding off of me like long pink worms. They keep me skinny. Worms are making me skinny and sleepy. Worms make me stay in bed. They tell me what to do. Eat, eat, they say and I do. They wait at the edge of my throat. I wait with mirror in hand. When it's very quiet, a little pink head sticks up and carries off a bit of food.

Ellen dreams of black crosses. Crosses made of twisted metal. Some are very thin, made thick only by coats of black paint. Beyond the crosses are headstones.
A new grave with the picture of a girl on it. A girl with pigtails holding a stuffed dog. She knew a girl once who got fat. One night she had a baby boy. She tried to flush him down the toilet but he was too solid. She left him in a dumpster.

The Story Of The Mayonnaise Man
There was a man who loved mayonnaise. He ate a jar full every day. One night he left the jar out on the table and in the morning it was full. He ate it and it was the best mayonnaise ever. He left the jar out again and the next morning it was full. He ate it and it was better than ever. One night he became curious and hid in the kitchen. He saw the door open and a man with an enormous sore walk in and squeeze pus into the jar.

Carl mesmerizes birds. He passes his hands three times over their bodies and they go still. He strokes the belly of a crawdad. It lies on its back in the cradle of his hand. He charms his boys. No more blows to the head. His work is clean and without surprise. He worked on a child using a bright light. He gave the body orders. He told it to become rigid and it did. The boy laid atop two chair backs as straight as an ironing board. He stuck a needle in a little at a time to test the trance. It went in under the eye socket one half inch.

He is grateful for the gift he has, the laying on of hands. The way his hands know the pull of the body. The magnetism that draws his fingers across the heat of the heart, lung and cock. How he knows later where the blood will gather beneath the buttocks and back, beneath the skin, cold and still and collected in a beautiful pool.

root

A root crooked and black was a beet but now hangs on fishing line embedded with metal to make a frame. A frame of a tiny heart which is the heart of Jesus lined up in a row of sacred beatings that pour forth blood and insects into basement apartments inhabited by single women living alone but together. Each room here is occupied with great rustling. Each room here is occupied with great desire.

the spaces for lovers to live in

Four floors above the escort parlor, the woman and the man went into a white room, all white, except for the yellow jam box he carried and then the pink of their bodies and then the black of their clothing that lay on the floor.

In London, in his brother's rented room, they lay on a single mattress. He asked her to wear the black high heels to bed and they placed a single carnation in an Ironman pop bottle.

In a tent, in an Irish field, the curves of their bodies were magnified and exaggerated by the torchlight, and the shadows thrown upon the green tent walls entertained the other campers.

When their money ran low they stayed in spaces only large enough to lay down in. They stayed in a car parked in a field with a lovely lake view ruined only by fishermen looking in.

They were together under a blanket at a public park wrapped up like a meat pie until cold weather set in.

They lived in the fruit bin of an icebox until the door was lawfully removed and left them exposed like a cross section of ripe melon.

They found shelter under a jumbo-sized paper cup that dissolved into soggy tissue during a rainstorm.

They were evicted from the back panel of a milk carton and replaced with dietary information and photos of missing children.

They moved into a bus locker until their allotted time was up and then they moved into a coin slot. Finally they lived on the head of a penny. Ironically, they argued over money. They separated, she stayed on the queen's shoulders, and he moved to the other side till a child found the penny in the dark corner where they had rolled it. He placed it on a track and the heat and weight of a train mashed the penny into a thin, copper spot.

psychic camp

The Strangest Occurrence in New Boston, Indiana
Two men lived together.

Some things told to me about the killer.

There were fires the summer before. The long dead grasses burned a small ring of fire around the block.

Small rings around the eyes of his ski mask.

His thefts were so bold. He would break into your house and wear your clothes around in front of you!
He slept during the day, he only came out at night going between the houses. One of the houses is grey dark asphalt siding virgin mary in front yard. The yard is small and bare, darkness there.

His child rides by on a bike with a banana seat.

What kind of killings would he do?

(Draw a map of the three houses)

Do a search in silence

What is your favorite memory?

The Man Who Came In Milk
There was a man named Crim who broke into women's houses and stole panties. He came in the milk. Everyone in Terre Haute said "fill it to the rim with Crim!"

A page of hair under tape (wide and clear).

A yearbook of Psychic Camp.
I'm alone in the group photo.

The underwear thief broke in and came on the bedspread. We cut the stain out and buried it. What can you do with a stain like that?

If the killer lives across the street from you what is the best way to proceed?

I proceed to date him.

They were getting out of the car. I said do you have ghosts here I said what dreams do you have here in this house haunted?

I say a killer. I say killer. I say killer now!

This is what you'll do at Psychic Camp. You'll play horseshoes and Gin Rummy, you'll read tarot cards and be visited by your spirit guides. You'll learn phrenology and moleosophy. You can practice on friends! You'll have a great time at Psychic Camp!

The psychic found the man missing in Kentucky. He'd gone bottle collecting at an old strip mine. She said he'd be near water. Lori knows the family of the girl missing from Carmi and they told her. This was not in the newspapers. This was not reported. This was not recorded. The psychic saw her in a building with high walls. Someone had taken her shoes. This was winter.

miriam

Miriam collects color pictures of outdoor scenes that light up. She has five mountain scenes, including one of a man panning for gold.

The pictures are photographs, blown up and placed on a screen. At night, she turns them all on and watches from her bed. It is like sleeping outside.

Miriam is forty and just divorced. She is living in an apartment so new that she does not know what the walls are made of.

While she has the money, she plays the tourist: visiting Buffalo Bill's grave, the railroad museum and playing slot machines in Central City.

Before she moved West, she lived on the Illinois prairie. When she looked at the sunset, she could see the Arch of St. Louis.

One time she rode to the top of the arch in a capsule which jerked on its chain. The arch swayed slightly in the wind. To look out of the windows, she had to lean forward and trust the thin metal to hold her.

Miriam forced herself to look below. She saw the city with its panorama of cars and people and factories that lay on the edges, then the brown farms and the blue skies of the West. All this while she floated above on the bones of a giant skeleton.

the rise of sex towards god

As a girl I imagined the sex of angels to be smooth hairless crotches such as the pink or black plastic doll flesh that rises under the mound of my hand. Beneath the other hand I feel the rise of my sex that pushes forward in an arch made visible by tight jeans. (I note in a journal the rise of my sex towards God).

Because the angels were created in my image, I assume them to possess coarse and dark crotches. Detailed like my own self which I no longer display naked in public except in grainy photographs. Like the portrait of my spirit guides I paid to have drawn in pastels. I sat for several hours as the artist meditated and sketched and then meditated and sketched. When I saw the finished portrait I was appalled to find that the artist had drawn an angel with an extremely large cock.

dream life in a case of transvestism

1

I'm in a man's uniform with military creases in the shirt. I search an informant for drugs or money, to verify that she goes in clean. It's very hot. She wears a tank top, shorts, and slip-on shoes. She pulls up her top; nothing beneath her breasts but a wire taped on for sound. I look down her shorts, pubic hair shaved. Check inside the soles of her shoes. Nothing. It's daylight and we are in an empty railroad yard.

2

My sister and I walk down the midway in matching sailor suits. My cousin Tommy is dressed in a nautical jacket, carrying a cane with a ceramic dalmatian head. All the carny barkers watch. They wish they were dressed like us.

3

At a party for girls only, I wear a can-can dress with big kittens on the skirt. It has a velcro zipper that I like to open and close. We take our clothes off. They all turn out to be boys. Later, I found out that I went on the wrong day.

4

I am a woman dressed as a man dressed as a woman. I am so much a woman I do not recognize myself. Yet I have never been more of a man.

My testicles lie beneath my skin and I touch the two knots in my groin. When I swear I place my right hand upon them and tell the truth, as told by me, a liar.

5

Since I became a woman dressed as a man dressed as a woman, I lost my virginity. There are sixteen types of hymens. I had thirteen of them. My hymen was a chameleon that hung from a chain on my sweater and changed shape constantly.

"What is that on your sweater?"

"It's just an old maidenhead that I spray painted gold and glued some sequins onto."

6

I lost it in a car in Kentucky, beneath the bridge where I was born in the car's back seat. My father drove, the doctor in back with my mother. My father drove faster and faster. Her pains came closer and closer together. The crown of my head emerged. We were late crossing the water. All of us were very, very late.

country

I don't know why we live like the poor. We are not poor like the Weber kids we used to pick up every Sunday and take to church. They were three boys with white hair and pale blue eyes that blinked constantly like three white mice and the girl had straight red hair chopped off at the ears. Before she grew up she was raped by her father and had his baby.

Many things are ugly about the country. Our neighbors, Tooties and Herb shot hogs in the head and hung them upside down on wooden crosses. The woman across the field chopped the heads off of chickens and let them chase us around the yard until they dropped over, then she ate them for dinner.

People who have always lived in the city think of the country as a refuge. I think of the city as a safe haven. In the city children run into the paths of cars. Here in the country, hunters flush deer out of the safe woods and into the path of your automobile and people stop to divide it into quarters while it's still warm.

In the country at night, airplanes ruin the view of the stars but I am happy to see them, happy that someone is going somewhere.

At dusk I have seen UFO's out here. My sister sees disembodied hands reaching for her out of the fog on our pond. My Grandma sees a man in Edwardian dress under the apple tree in the backyard.

I moved back here in November, when the fields were brown and dead and the tracks of farmers and deer were laid clear. I am thirty years old and pregnant. Maybe I will have to get married like the lunch counter girl in high school, who only did it once. She stayed in school getting larger everyday as a testament to sin.

In school I was a virgin and had terrible dreams of being pregnant and not being able to explain it and knowing that I had to become my mother. It was like that one dream of coming to school naked and no one tells you and you realize it during class. You know you're not to blame but no one believes you.

I am at home again after being gone since eighteen and I am working in my parents' store. They don't mind that I'm with child and the father left me; they're just glad it isn't AIDS.

I am four months along. I wear baggy clothes so the customers who knew me as a girl won't ask why I'm back. Do they want to know I failed? Twelve years have passed but I am still a girl to them. Our store is six miles down the road from our house. I drive down the same gravel roads I saw from the school bus window every day in grade school. I pass through bean and corn fields that surround the farmhouses. In the growing season, corn is all you can see. You are encircled by it.

I pass the Weber house on the way. It is an asphalt sided shotgun with chickens scratching in the dirt and a few outbuildings. I wonder about the girl that grew up there. I wonder how she felt carrying her father's baby? Did she love the baby? How could she love it?

Her father used to come into the store and buy groceries. He was skinny and unshaven but he had good credit and worked on a chicken farm. Her mother had a baby the same year her daughter did and named it after a soap opera star, one to whom bad things always happened.

In the store there is a drink box, a meat counter and two shopping carts. The floors are oiled and we burn cardboard boxes in a Franklin stove. Across the street is an old garage that is covered in license plates lined up in sequence by year and color. People come from miles around to see it and the Sunday drivers who would like to stay (but have more places to see) think they have found Utopia.

There are three churches here. The Pentecostal church has a boy preacher. He is on fire for the Lord and asks if he can leave religious tracts on the counter. I went to school with his father. They are all named Ronnie, even the grampa and they are all preachers except for a sister, Ellen, who left half eaten bags of cookies hidden behind the canned goods.

They built themselves a new parsonage with the money they earned preaching and the grandfather died of a heart attack soon after and that left two preachers in the family. I know what became of them because I see their names on the church marquee. But I never knew what was going on at the Weber house until I read about it in the paper and she was sent away and he was arrested.

The boys come up to our house and buy junk cars from my father. I wonder what they think? Do they ever see her? Their adult heads are elongated and their bodies are tall and narrow. They live across the road from their dad in a big house that used to be for foster children. Sometimes they come into the store and buy a jug of milk. One day, I will ask them what happened to her and they will go out to the car and bring in a redheaded child and say, "This is the baby."

They are collecting cardboard boxes. They are going to paint them black and put wheels on them. They are making baby coffins to pull in a parade. They are digging graves a foot long and a foot wide. They are calling it a cemetery for the unborn.

They ask me for boxes and I say, "No, I don't have any," then burn all the extra boxes in the stove. I have seen what they do to women. The women of their church cover every loin and calf with long skirts and every neck with a high collar.

The Ronnies are preparing for the parade. The grand marshal is a man who is walking across this country with a giant cross on his back. There is a picture of him in the newspaper, dragging a cross beneath a palm in California. He says his back is scarred from splinters but he is driven by the pain, as it brings him closer to the suffering of Jesus Christ. He visits churches and preaches to pay his way. He only needs some food and little shelter. He is going to write a book about his journey when he is done but keeps no notes. God speaks to him and will gift him with the words he needs.

Lights are strung up along the parade route which ends at the store. I have been driving these cold nights along county roads and coming upon a white frame house with no door, only plastic covering the frame and under the yellow bug light the words, "No Trespassing" are painted on the wall. The farmers say the Weber girl lives there.

I hear the grade school marching band coming up the street playing Christmas carols with their blue lips and fingers. They are followed by Baby Jesus in the manger and a pickup truck filled with children dressed as presents and a sign proclaiming them the "Joys of Christmas."

I watch from the window and I see the Ronnies coming. They are pulling the boxes and carrying signs handwritten in a childish scrawl that say "Save Me." I wish I could show them a picture of a woman, dead and naked as seen from behind on her knees and blood caked in dry streams from her vagina to the floor. Following them is a float with a man strapped to a cross and a Roman soldier carrying a silver shield made from a beaten serving platter. He is mocking the dying Jesus. The Jesus imitator is wearing a loincloth. On the sides of the float are banners with two large palms with spikes driven through them and dripping blood drawn on them and the words, "The True Meaning of Christmas." Behind the float, the Grand Marshal bears his cross. He is followed by a woman who has fashioned one for herself from scraps of lumber.

The Marshal is wearing a robe and dress shoes. She is wearing a purple cloak. They stop in front of the license plates and the boy preacher places a crown of thorns upon the Marshal's head and the woman washes his feet with her hair. I come out from behind the screen door of the store. I touch her red hair and pull her up from her knees and the hand I pull is pitted and wet with burns and jagged cuts from the sliver of mirror in her palm. "Come here," I say and press her hand to my body. Her eyes never reach mine. They are lost in the rapture of tongues and atonement.

ostriches running

Ostriches Running: Part One

The film opens with a man running alone in a corral. Suddenly the corral is filled with ostriches running along side him.

Ostriches Running: Part Two

A man is running alone in a corral. Suddenly the corral is filled with ostriches running along side him.

Ostriches Running: Part Three

The film opens with a man running towards a group of chickens causing them to stampede.

appendage

My brother took $4000 to the carnival and came home with two ostriches. He says they're the other white meat. He says special slaughterhouses are being built. He says it's the newest in meat. He says it's the new meat.

blackie

My dog Blackie dances for me every evening for treats. Her teeth are rotten, worn down to black and brown stumps. She dances on the spindle-legged table under a picture of the Lord's Supper, even on Sundays.

My son eats squirrel brains in the kitchen. He deep fries them and cracks open the skulls and sucks them down while his lungs fill. I pound his back pound that gunk right out of him.

This morning, Blackie was in the garden being charmed by a snake. The snake did his dance on Blackie. I said, "Snake, your eyes are bigger than your head. Your belly bulges and I will cut you open and let out all the frogs, mice and rabbits in there."

At night, my son lies on his bed. I hear the rale of his lungs, the soft drowning in his sleep. His breaths keep me up. I count his breaths like sheep. During my dreams, snakes are in my bed rising up at me. I burn them in the trash heap. Their bodies crackle and twist, they rise up like devils trying to talk sweet in the flames.

When my boy is well, he hunts in the woods around our house. He waits there for squirrels and rabbits. He tracks the rabbits back to their holes: so quiet even his lungs barely whisper. He used to bring home the small brown babies for pets. I wonder how he can take their lives so easily.

Blackie dances well for an old dog, 14 years old and hardly any fur. I crank the gramophone, Blackie dances on two legs practically begging. I take her paws and my boy comes in from the kitchen and joins us. We all begin howling. We howl and howl again and all because we can.

margaret

Every day, Margaret and her monkey go to the baby show to look for Margaret's daughter. The monkey is on a leash and very well trained. He is not allowed to touch any glass.

Hanging on the outside of the show tent are paintings of the babies: the cyclops child, the lamb-headed boy, the twins joined at the waist, the lizard-faced girl.

The paintings are large and bright.

The show is owned by two men who are lovers. Every day the female one dusts the jars and checks their fluid levels. They live in a trailer behind the tent. The trailer is full of small dogs they breed to sell.

Margaret dances in *The Arabian Nights* show. She stands on a platform at show time and shimmies in her harem outfit, made of chiffon veils and lined with gold coins. Her monkey rides on her shoulders and unhooks the colored layers during her dance.

Margaret stares at the baby jars and wonders if one of them were taken out, would he or she be rubbery like a rotten egg. The babies' faces are pressed up against the glass. In the bigger jars, some of them float up to the top as if to take a breath and then dive to the bottom.

Sometimes pieces break off of the older ones and sink to the bottom. The men use a long handled spoon to scoop up the fragments.

Margaret's lover is Mike the Mouse. He entices the marks to play. He says, "Come on in and win you one, come on in and win."

The mice are all white and come from a pet store. He uses one per night. The mouse runs into a numbered hole, sometimes it is stunned. He shakes a stick at it until it moves.

The prizes are stuffed animals.

On their mattress, in the bed of the hoochie-coochie wagon, he says to Margaret, "Come on in and win."

Each tear-down night, the two men pack the jars between newspapers to cushion the ride. They roll up the canvas and everything folds in upon itself.

Sometimes Margaret sees a new one or notices one in the back behind the other jars. She wonders where all the babies come from.

Her own baby was a lion-faced girl with a split lip that curled up on the edges. The doctor showed her and took the girl away.

The father was Arlo the gypsy boy. He lived in a trailer with his family. All the children slept on cots outside. He was the milk bottle man. He said, "Knock 'em over and win. Knock 'em over and win."

No one could knock the bottles down. They were filled with weights.

He said to Margaret in the top booth of the empty grandstand, "You knock me over."

Margaret wears a dress made of mirrors. She's a tourist attraction; a reflecting pool of human wonder.

tinderbox

In the town she lives as the wealthiest woman in the house she inherited from her father. The house is filled with Bavarian cuckoo clocks that coo on the hour and the half hour. The woman is thin, thinner than a blade of grass and her daughter is thinner than bones. Her daughter is skin that covers a skeleton. This is the only house the woman hasn't burned down by falling asleep while smoking. The house is on a hill across from the nunnery where she went to school. The woman is glad to be living here close to the end of her life, otherwise this house would have been torched already; especially since it is such a tinderbox.

At her wedding she wore a dirndl and her husband wore lederhosen and a felt wool hat with dark feathers and colored badges. At the biergarden everyone sang from song sheets because only their fathers knew German. They toasted with green stemmed glasses.

Her daughter lives in an apartment below the hill, in the belly of the town. Her apartment is long and not wide. Her movements can be traced by the flicking on and off of lights at night. She is balding so she dyes her hair with black shoe polish which she sponges on to cover the pink of her scalp. She is young and not ill. Her hair is not the thick blond hair of farm girls even though she was conceived in a corn crib. She thinks of the summer crops pushing through the cracks of the wooden slats and her parents getting long cuts from the stalks. Her hair is tender corn silk.

When she was little she used to visit the nunnery and stare at the hair wreaths the nuns wove from the tresses cut off after their vows. She remembers singeing her hair in the first fire, and the smell of burning books and bibles from the high and low countries in their smoky attic.

Her father was raised at the abbey where the monks made home brew and paid cash for everything. They milked the cows at midnight on Saturdays to keep holy the Sabbath day. They made soup from the turtles they fattened up in drum barrels. He wore a cassock even to plow in and spent his days in the gardens and at the dairy praying.

When he was a boy he had a vision of a heart encircled with thorns and a blazing cross rising from the top of it. He drew it on every scrap of paper he found. Hearts encircled with thorns, flaming hearts like firm, ripe tomatoes.

Her mother met him at the nunnery where she went to school. Later she thought it was his long tunics that attracted her; all those layers to get beneath to reach bare skin. It was the first time he had been where the air smelled of women. He was her teacher. She was 15, the town doctor's daughter.

They married and lived in a farmhouse with two front doors and a porch. He taught school and she lived as a wife sewing all the rags into rugs, melting all the fat into soap. She learned broken Deutsche from the farm wives. When their daughter was born, they rocked her every night in a wooden cradle. The woman put sage in her daughter's bed to keep evil away. She checked the pillows in the house for pinwheels; even a clump of feathers alarmed her, for the farm wives told her it means death.

She fell asleep smoking and they got out coughing and singed. This is when God began to call him.

God's voice is like a tea kettle singing. A soft whistle that grows shrill. God sang, "Your pillows are soft, your wife so lovely, your daughter so tender."

He made his wife put away worldly things and to cover her head.

"Do you hear that?" he said. His limbs grew heavy. He drank only warm milk from a teaspoon. He drew his picture over and over again, trying to burn God's heart into his memory.

The daughter remembers him urging her to eat only the Eucharist and to take only tea.

"I wanted the milk of his attention," she said. She sewed Christ's name in the dead skin of her heel and covered her fingers and palms with candle wax. The little pains she could do, the large ones she could not. She did them on farm animals, bugs, toads, and birds. She severed their limbs one by one. She gave the hogs last rites on butchering day. "Bless this liver sausage and bratwurst," she said.

Her mother said, "Most daughters are angels, mine is a ghoul."

"I was a hog in another life," the girl said, "I lived in a shack and my mother ate the afterbirth off of me. That is how much a mother can love you. One day, the farmer came to get one of us to butcher. I was the fattest so he took me. From that life I learned to be thin. Then I was a deer springing across a field and following the run through the thicket. I had a beautiful white tail that I would lift up until I was shot. From that life I learned not to be proud."

In the house, the woman winds the clocks, she waits for him to stop breathing. She said, "He married me because he was afraid to marry God."

After he died, she made a fire of her dresses and his drawings and crosses. Her daughter singed the hair on her head and arms pulling the charred crosses out of the flames.

nature

I am removed from nature. I left the farm, the udders, the sour smells.

Our farm where everything lived in cages. The little chicks and rabbits dropped their turds through the wire mesh. When I was there I was caged in our house and our church. My bed, I shared with my sister. Oh, the dreams, where I rolled over and tried to kiss her because my dreams of touching men were so strong that I thought she was one.

"Father, your daughter dreams of touching each night. All of that dreaming is fraying the sheets."

My father was the executioner. He wrapped the frayed cord around Blackie's neck. He filleted the fish. He dressed the deer. He jointed the bunnies and rolled them in the flour. He drove the wheelbarrow to the smoke house. He cured the ham that was cut from the tender thighs of our pets.

When I was there, I took on the body of a dog, a dog on its hind legs, doing tricks, begging perhaps, stealing, or speaking. My bony chest stuck out and my pelvis became hollow. I spoke in short, quick bursts. I was only missing the long rows of nipples.

I left that farm, where calves were fattened and offered up. I was a dumb and shoeless beast clothed in velvety rags. I walked for days, living in fields and orchards. Eating vegetables from gardens, my movement as nimble as a deer's.